D1231947

Volume 74 of the Yale Series of Younger Poets

Leslie Ullman

Natural Histories

Foreword by Richard Hugo

New Haven and London
Yale University Press

Published with assistance from
the Mary Cady Tew Memorial Fund.

Designed by Sally Harris
and set in Monotype Bembo type
by Heritage Printers, Inc., Charlotte, N.C.
Printed in the United States of America by
The Murray Printing Company, Westford, Mass.

Published in Great Britain, Europe, Africa, and
Asia (except Japan) by Yale University Press,
Ltd., London. Distributed in Australia and
New Zealand by Book & Film Services, Artarmon,
N.S.W., Australia; and in Japan by Harper & Row,
Publishers, Tokyo Office.

Library of Congress Cataloging in Publication Data

Ullman, Leslie.
  Natural histories.

  (Yale series of younger poets ; v. 74)
  I. Title. II. Series.
PS3571.L57N3   811'.5'4   78-25591
ISBN 0-300-02329-4
ISBN 0-300-02330-8 pbk.

For Rush

Contents

Foreword

When John Keats defined negative capability, the poet's capability "of being in uncertainties, mysteries, doubts, without any irritable reaching after fact and reason," he might have foreseen a poet like Leslie Ullman. I'm sure he would have admired her work, but he might have been mystified by it and found himself wondering if he hadn't been defining not the capability of the poet but the capability needed by the audience.

For Ullman writes in such a matter-of-fact way that the "uncertainties" seem like certainties, with events and responses often peripheral and removed from context, but readily accepted. The mysteries seem solved and Ullman seems to have no doubts. Yet they remain uncertainties, mysteries, and doubts in the reader, at least on first reading. Consequently, her poems are all the more fascinating.

It is as if an assured, astute, direct woman began talking in a down-to-earth way about both her own experiences and those from the lives of others. We would find ourselves so impressed by her lack of affectation we'd know she was telling us the truth. But the truth would seem so unusual as it came out that the contrast between her level voice and the strangeness of her utterances would only compound the mysteriousness of the occasion.

Music is often the only thing a poet can depend on for help during the composition of a poem. For poets of the strange, the music is often imposing (Dylan Thomas, Theodore Roethke), just as for fiction writers the narrative is often bizarre (Franz Kafka). Ullman's music is so unobtrusive that the ear picks it up but may not recognize that it is there. It is far easier to admire her poems and marvel at them than to discuss them. She heightens the dramatic impact by her tone, which subtly insists the poems are not dramatic. They are very dramatic, even if the big

scenes do occur off-camera, since often her effects are like those
details we remember from a movie long after we've forgotten
the plot.

To Ullman both isolation and togetherness contain paradoxes
that can be accepted and never resolved. (She can accept any-
thing because to her nothing is irrelevant.) People are present
when absent and absent when present. In "Beyond Dreams,"
the woman prepares for her rendezvous by rehearsing both roles,
hers and the man's, complete with responses. When the man
comes, filled with his own fantasies of what his needs are and
what she will do to fulfill them, the woman is more removed
from him than she was before he arrived. They are intimate
when separated. Together they are remote from one another.
That's not so odd when we think about how many people we
know who seem to marry in order to have someone not to
talk to.

Complementing the paradox of isolation and intimacy is the
paradox of distance and immediacy. "On Vacation a Woman
Mistakes Her Leg" sketches a world where imagined relation-
ships are idealized by distant observers into something real while
real relationships are weakened and even at moments falsified by
the immediacy of the protagonists.

Ullman ranges from third to second to first person and back
again. That's not simply gratuitous grammatical travel. She often
finds it necessary to journey out of herself into other bodies and
other selves in order to write. Sometimes she relies solely on her-
self, certain that she is whatever has happened to her and that
whatever has happened to her is licensed for inclusion in the
poem. Examples include "Characters," "Proof," "The Friends
I Had as a Child," and "Integumentary."

"Integumentary" is a sort of aesthetic creed, a faith that covers
one of her processes of writing, covers it like a "skin, membrane,
or husk" if we go to the dictionary for the definition of *integu-
ment*. After establishing a set of rules for herself in a voice remi-

niscent of Polonius, in her own voice she lists the results of obey-
ing those rules. There are some confusions of identity,

> You may be someone you met somewhere,
> you can no longer tell

and confusions between inner and outer worlds, between mental
and physical acts,

> You no longer know a difference
> between question and travel

but the rewards are worth it:

> you could weave yourself into any location
> if you stayed long enough.
> You court everything.
> You pull out words
> where you can. Wherever you reach
> you touch a cheek, a chin, a wild eye
> you've known well.

I said "one of her processes." She is no more consistent than is
anyone who honestly follows the contours of the mind. In
"Memo" she rejects what has happened to her as a source of
poems and relies on a self that remains unchanged by the im-
pact of experience. Here she depends on her relation with lan-
guage because it is an important part of her relation to herself,
and so carries the longest history of trust.

When the self can't be relied on, in the interests of creativity
she creates a second self and enters into it with seemingly little
fear—not as easy a matter as it might look. In "Why There Are
Children" urges to another self, to a better world, to regress to
a better time, become the same urge, the urge to conceive. Why
are there children? For the same reason there are memories and
dissatisfactions and idealizations and delusions and poems.

Ullman often travels backward, perhaps hoping to demon-

strate the truth of the epigraph from Kierkegaard in "The Im-
maculate Stairs": "The piece of music must be played through
backwards; otherwise the enchantment is not broken." I re-
main unconvinced that the enchantment is broken, enchanted
as I am by the poem. In "The Woman at the Desk" an unful-
filled woman travels back to "some other life" where "men
guarded their women with spears" and "she slipped away at
dawn / scarcely disturbing the thick branches." A poem is cre-
ated out of the bare details at the edges of a whole novel that
remains unwritten.

She is capable of teasing us with who she would like to be,
experiences she would like to have, and with the world as she
would like it: "Plumage," for example. Her poems are enriched
and made more complete by our responses, and while that is a
risky process, she is a poet worthy of it because she can turn
many of us into worthy readers.

Most of all, Ullman is a winner. She wins out over the tyranny
art imposes on our vision of the world ("In Barcelona You
Tried to Scream"). She wins out over the memories that jeop-
ardize our impulse to love ("L'Étriente") and the fears we re-
hearse to ensure that we're ready to cope with life. She wins be-
cause she receives reality with patience and does not struggle
against her chains only to have them tighten all the more. She
waits for the right phrase, utters that phrase, and the chains slip
off.

One of her victories of special importance to poets is won in
her unusual poem "His Early and Late Paintings," a poem about
—among other things—the reciprocal relation of art and ex-
perience. In the poem, paintings without titles reduce the viewer
to conjecture about the experience behind the paintings. Once
the reviewer reacts to his own reactions to the paintings them-
selves, he can stop asking biographical questions about the paint-
er, and in place of the questions provide titles to the paintings.
So just as titles, or names of things, tend to direct or manage

our responses to the things themselves, our responses, apprehended and acknowledged, can help create names of things. For most poets, it's a faith hard to do without.

Ullman is a poet of confinement and release, of restriction and freedom. She does not bother, thankfully, to separate exterior and interior reality. If one woman is too limited by quotidian existence to energize language, the other woman inside quitely takes over and locates the fresh paths that lead to the realization of the complete poem. If immediate reality is too limp for the poem's design, Ullman's long and patient gaze will find something beyond the limits of normal vision that will make the poem firm.

In her honest, quiet way, Ullman puts to poetic use the self-generating power that lies within her. No restraint is so permanent it cannot be cast off, no confinement so total release cannot be won. Her freedom is the ideal freedom of the poet: the mind going on, distilling, adding, converting, supplementing and complementing, certain of the real relationship of response to event no matter how remote or peripheral the events are or how ineffectual or unrelated the responses seem. Reading *Natural Histories* many times, I've come to feel her freedom is my freedom.

Richard Hugo

Acknowledgments

Acknowledgment is made to the following magazines for poems, or earlier forms of poems, originally published in them.

Antioch Review: "In Barcelona You Tried to Scream"
Ark River Review: "Bravado," "Breakfast," "By Surprise,"
  "Money," "Rain," "Undressing," "Waiting"
Carleton Miscellany: "Beyond Dreams"
Cincinnati Poetry Review: "Reunions"
Epoch: "Integumentary," "Memo"
Mademoiselle: "Plumage"
Montana Gothic: "The Woman at the Desk" (under the title,
  "Circles")
The Nation: "Eventually, You," "His Early and Late Paintings."
New Letters: "Proof"
The New Yorker: "On Vacation a Woman Mistakes Her Leg,"
  "Why There Are Children"
Open Places: "Ceremony," "The Immaculate Stairs," "Nostal-
  gia," "Routes"
Poetry Northwest: "Characters," "Health"
Seneca Review: "Shade," "The Voyeurs"
Shenandoah: "A Prefiguration"

I am especially grateful to the National Endowment for the Arts for a grant which gave me time and encouragement to complete this book.

I

Last Night They Heard the Woman Upstairs

moaning. They lay in bed
and she did not stop

and she did not stop, and she did not
grow louder.

The husband saw her once, moonfaced
and ample on the stairs.

The wife did not move
her hand along his thigh,

the short hairs springing there.
For a moment she pictured him

not in the bed, not alive
and a scream cracking

like some withered thing from her lips.
Tonight the husband is reading.

The wife bites into a peach.
The woman upstairs

slams a door. The building
takes back its silence like breath.

Last night they heard her
moaning, and they waited

3

and they thought their skin was visible
through the sheets and the drawn

shade. And the husband said,
She must make love slowly, the way

she climbs the stairs.

In Barcelona You Tried to Scream

to Susan

You had spent the day looking at paintings.
The real park was too green, still dappled
at twilight. The crippled children sat
too quietly. Someone had dressed them
in lace and gabardine, like the antique
figures you'd seen through a haze of fatigue.
You covered your daughter's eyes.
You stared at the children under the trees
who stared at nothing, their incurable lives.
Their deaths seemed to rise inside them
like the sleep of the newly-born.
Their nurse gazed over the pond.
Your husband said JUST DRIVE
and you held the wheel like a pair of shoulders.

Tonight you dine in Paris. Without turning
you know the street outside glitters,
that people speak cheerfully into the wind.
If you close your eyes, you can see the women's
faces floating like orchids. Your husband
offers you a light, and you lean forward
in your fragile chair, in the middle of Paris.
In an invisible France, people you'll never meet
are lighting lamps for their frightened children,
or driving too fast, or selling everything.
In Barcelona you tried to scream.
In Paris your husband offers you a light
and his hands carve themselves in one motion
behind your eyes.

Why There Are Children

The woman inside every woman
lights the candles.
This is the woman sons look for

when they leave their wives.
Daughters become wives
thinking they travel backward

to the dresser covered with lace,
the hairpins still scattered there
and the cameo earrings.

The same gnarled tree
darkens the bedroom window.
The hair coiled in a locket

conceals the hands of men and children.
When a woman shivers on the porch,
perhaps at dusk, it is the other

wanting a shawl. When a woman
in her middle years rises
and dresses for work, the other

reaches for the cameos
remembering a great love
and herself on the brink of it.

Midwife

She smells blood in her hair
and dreams of crouching at the limits
of her skin. Having spent themselves
the new mothers sleep like men
in the scent of what they are.

The pain, she thinks, is the
first scream to dismantle itself.
They did not try to swallow
her hands, small awed husbands.
Each speaks softly, on two legs,
as if the room had been lit by candles.

It is she who reels in the corridor.
They smell of flowers. They say:
It was only the body emptying itself.

Characters

At the crosswalk they will take your arm,
guessing your feet want to stick to the curb
and the city does not open itself.

They will lead you between buildings
where the windows let in air and the women
are humming, their shoes kicked aside.

They will show you the broken parts
of fences. Each tiny lawn. They will tell you
what they do in spite of themselves and joyfully

behind their doors. Your toes will begin to
loosen and the streets let you go. On each block
you'll notice flights of stairs.

They will guide you to a table, order the specialty
and murmur where each person outside
has been. You'll protest, you'll not believe it

all; you will find yourself leaning
forward, shrugged free of your manners,
the day polished off with the meal.

They will leave soon; you'll not see them
grow old. Back on the streets you'll move
with the parcels, the thoughts that occur,

the lights that break up the evening.

The Sunday Dialogues

1

Two men: one drains his glass,
one eyes a placid
woman crossing unremarkable legs.
One says he only imagines his hands
on the thighs of women half-
asleep, who slowly feel his damp skin.
One says,
"I tear off their clothes."

2

The woman I have become
crosses her legs
and stares at newsprint on a page,
a strand of hair,
her glass suddenly empty.
He tears off their clothes.
I cross my legs.

3

He would tear off her clothes.
She stares out the window
as if waiting to breathe.
His hips would move fast as a boy's.
She hears him explain an idea
has walls, and floors below ground.
His hips would move faster
than she remembers later.

4

One says young girls imagine themselves
more real than their mothers
who retire calmly at night in flannel gowns.

5

The other
surrounds her
as though each of his limbs were a body.

6

Or does he brush
each of her fingers
gently?

7

Surely she moves
and forces him to dance:
Does he wave his arms and say, "Darling?"
Do his hands close and open against his will?
Who removes the water and the broken glass?

8

At the next table, a woman
crosses and recrosses
her legs. A stone on a chain hangs
between the waitress's breasts.
A single stone, warm as a finger, sinks
and rises as she hands him a glass.

Proof

They meet under a speckled canopy
of moonlight;
I am their daughter.

The little girl on their wall grins.
I am the woman in the spare room
peeling off gloves, boots, admiring
my invisible body.

I look like the mistress of the house
when I leave the room. My absence
lacks a shape of its own.

Have I ever lived alone?

I have forgotten
none of my grievances.
The lobster is superb,
as is the orchestra, each member
perspires in his tuxedo.

Soon I will let myself back into the street.
A friend will speak of his father's huge hands.
I will enter my parents' house over & over.
I will eat oranges until my skin is flawless.

Fur

The small boy at dusk
arranges himself in the dark

bones of a tree.
Moths enter the blue air

and come home. His mother leans
into it, calling his name. Her body

smells like milk. Behind her
the moon climbs like a slow howl

and his father comes home
swollen or in pain

resting on the last few stairs.
His voice breaks into the small room.

Listening, the boy finds no place
for so many words

and later his mother's kiss
adheres to him like fur.

He kicks off the sheets
and hears nothing.

Two eyes touch
the length of him through branches.

A long way in, he hears
his parents breathe through their skin.

Long vowels uncurl in their throats.
He hears his name

as less than sound,
a slight movement of wings.

Beyond Dreams

She felt free—but there was nothing she could do about it.
                                                    —Peter Handke

She calls on herself.
She loosens her hair
before the woman in the mirror who smiles
as the man would smile
at such long hair.
She picks up a shell that seems to pull
the walls of the room
toward itself
like a woman carrying a child.
She touches it
as she might touch every part
of the man's body.

At dusk
she eats as though someone else is eating,
as though the man has poured the wine
and she has brought them
into a safe hunger.

And when the man arrives
looking for someone slender,
someone smelling of petals,
someone whose hands might follow the curve
of his great sadness

he finds strands of long hair in the brush,
long dresses in the closet,
himself in the mirror with a young girl
who keeps rising to touch books and small objects,
who keeps looking out the window
as if someone were waiting.

A Prefiguration

Sometimes you swim to me,
gliding over these buildings
in old coat. You wait at the light
where I'm caught beyond the view from every
window. For a moment I'm like no one else
and you put a hand on my shoulder.

We watch my bus pull away
from the curb. We measure perfect distance
behind the boss unlocking the rooms of a lovely
secret acquaintance. Wearing opera glasses
we attend a display of somber biographies
and later the food and the usual stories.

But when the subject turns to money
and it's my voice that floats above the crystal,
you leave a space shaped into the span
of shoulders, cool as the glass
in my hand. And suddenly I see the wrists
below the sleeves of my disguise.

I remove old woolens from their airtight wrappings
and I leave for the country.
I let you out like a handful of moths.
If someone listens while I wait for rain
to stop, or a ride to appear,
it is not you.

The Friends I Had as a Child

call and call their children.
They nail down carpets.
At night I hear the leaves
settling on their lawns.
And the assistants, the typists—this morning
their faces have not closed yet.
They have been seen in brilliant shirts.
They have climbed the steps of distant monuments.
Their hands shake as they write their memoirs.

I swallow coffee and remember semen
in my mouth. How I cupped my hands.
The pale streetlamps at dawn.
On the train, like a child
I forget where I live.
I watch men and women parting
in tears. Later I am startled
by the stillness of their sleep
and the scent I've been wearing for hours.

The Voyeurs

Beyond our table the waitress hid the smile
her mother may have worn before the war.
Each of the calm patrons revealed a tic,

a sleeve, a secret fondness
for knees. When we murmured
names, they offered blond children,

a turquoise sea, an actor's autograph.
Perhaps our lives resembled these.
But for a flaw of imagination, we might have left

on the arm of a woman who in our presence
would abandon herself.
From the street we noted a bit of silk or smoke

and granted the people awake in their homes
our loneliness, our love of interiors.
Their lamps startled us. We longed for sleep.

The couple on the sofa would never remember
their wariness. In his study the father
straightened his robe, passing a night

remote and inevitable as the history
of our ancestors
who avoided all reference to the body.

Plumage

A woman will appear in place of light
wearing the colors
she wore while a man
reached toward her one night
at a time.

Others will find the flower at her throat,
small fires in the cave of her hair,
and one will rise to a dance
which may stop at the end of the room,
which may stop if somebody speaks.
His hands will tell her
she is the last of a kind.

She will free her breasts
which grew magnificent
in a mirror
while boys gathered in dark barns.
Her hands will tell of a room
she once knew. The curve
of the bowl on the table.

His hands will search
as though a door might open the way
to the stranger inside him.
He will keep the secrets
men tell and tell in the dark.

In town he will drive past
a window full of dresses
handed down by women who left messages
in the hand of one man
in the half-light
of one cabaret
at a time.

She will know a woman going home at night
could be going into any room, some arrangement
of light, some manner of remembering.

Once upon a time
a man noticed how a dress touched
every rib of a woman breathing
years after she rose from the table.

Nostalgia

The old man who told us all he knew
has not been seen.
The shops offer thin sweaters.
The entire population
has forgotten how the bodies of its women
emerge at night before sleep.
They once strolled across the quay
or a sunlit room
and decided to stay.

*

Inland the lights go out
and a child's parents
call to one another
across an extra room.
Across the silence
of the house at certain hours.
The children
move into our bodies.

*

I heard you listening
to the murmur of her absence,
to the murmur of fame,
to the murmur of women turning in their sleep
in rooms where they'd wake alone,
to the murmur of leaves outside the house
you should have lived in.

*

When it rained I followed the streets
until the women leaned from windows.
The children went inside.
The men who had been away all day
went inside, and old stories
rose in me like prophecies.

*

At night we unpacked everything.
The marks on our skin never changed.
The warm weather returned,
the cathedral
was aired for the strangers
who would arrive in light clothing,
who would cross themselves
and peel oranges outside the gates.

The Immaculate Stairs

The piece of music must be played through backwards;
otherwise the enchantment is not broken.

—Kierkegaard

Her bedroom smelled of trees.
A grey woman who was not her mother
waited with the gown and warm milk.
While she slept, a stranger
let himself into the white rooms below
and touched everything
silver. The full moon pulled
at the woman inside her
skin. It whitened.

*

At night he passed through rooms
so large they seemed to be empty.
His arms filled the dark sleeves.
The moonlight touched his hands,
his face in the urn's surface.
Upstairs, the silk against her skin
deafened him. The silk against her skin
drowned the voices of thieves.

*

As the sun reached the curve
of the spoon on the white cloth
she rose.
She picked up the spoon.
She began to grow plump.

*

She rose
and went down to the garden.
The immaculate stairs. Branches
sheltered the stone bench.
As the silk fell from her shoulders
someone spoke her mother's name.
A shaft of sun crossed
her grandmother's thin chain.
The man she had been expecting seized
her hand, only her hand
and said, "You are
lovely."

The Woman at the Desk

The woman at the desk answers the phone
and remembers nothing.
She has put her breasts to sleep.
Loose blouse, a rope of pearls,
the cup of hot milk. In the morning
the sheets are scarcely wrinkled.
She dives into the pearls.
All day they rise and fall.

*

She removes each garment
from the skin she's always worn,
from the body he left quietly
eating his soup
and growing thinner.
She kicks off her shoes.
In someone else's youth
men guarded their women with spears.

*

While she sleeps, an immense
darkness gathers beneath her skin.
The small house
holds off the invisible hands.
Sometimes she dreams of a man's arm
around her shoulders.

*

Stuffed against the coat
her breasts want to be naked.
They bloom here
as though they lived in the tropics.
In some other life she traveled light.
In some other life she slipped away at dawn
scarcely disturbing the thick branches.

Bravado

I should have been
one of those lean
women seen up
and down the coast

with neat gin.
A long story.
By mistake I live
miles from water

and do not smoke. This
man on the saxophone
moans, and plans
his journey someplace

else; his cheeks swell
as though pushing
sound through sea
air and old money.

He doesn't under-
stand: there is no war
anywhere, no veranda,
no bravado of sons about

to leave; that I am
a woman with no ear
for an old story;
that my cheek sags

when touched; that there
are no more bad nights;
that another year
has fattened and passed without

smudging my unastonished eye.

Screens

Every man in this room is tired
even of women he can't have.
That's what I thought.
You would have brought champagne.
You would have offered me a glass
on the porch, which was too cold
for the others. I drank nothing.
I nibbled the gourmandise.
We would have watched the frozen screens
scatter light from the street
and I would have murmured, *Champagne*
looks like people fleeing a scene.
The new year arrived
and then another, and you weren't
there. Everyone touched his glass
to someone's glass. Some kissed
as if kissing wet glass.
In the kitchen, the possibility
was this: you leaned on my shoulder
and I felt all of my luminous bones.
Using your hands, and the air between us,
you described the small, perfect
breasts of the women you've loved.

Breakfast

Your husband has just thrown a cup.
Your kitchen fills with sunlight.

Your hands grow
massive, capable of anything.

The folds of his beard
arrange themselves over the mouth

inside, the real mouth that never
moves. He sits down

and you face one another
and you see nothing, like people

who sit down in public.
The cup's round sides crash

gently behind your eyes. *Again and again
you come down to the cold kitchen*

and watch the steam rise from his hands.
He emptied the cup, standing at the window.

You came downstairs
thinking at first the room was empty.

You had dreamed you weren't dreaming
as he traced the line where the dark

flame of your hair touched
his face. The cup hit the floor.

Now the house shifts its weight.
The ferns in the window darken

and melt, and soon he will disappear
as usual, for good.

Your daughter enters the kitchen
not fully awake, her bare feet

missing the barely visible pieces.

Distraction

The night my eldest sister
fled, plans for a duel
floated over the table
with the burgundy in green glass.
The jellies glowed on earthenware.
The lovely pain, murmured Mother,
not thinking of her cold lungs
but the snow, and a soldier she had
barely known, growing cold in it.
I began to notice our ancestors

sneaking in at night with the china
and the warm stones. They laid their
cold breath across the coals
and made Mother's red gown rise,
empty, behind my closed lids.
This will make you sleep, Mother
said, bending all of herself over the spoon.
As I shut my eyes, Father spoke
of his first doe: . . . *the mist at dawn
made the spruces float above the clearing.*

That winter the drifts grew into walls
which glowed, nights, beyond the gauze
curtains. They curled in the heat of Mother's
fever; she thought they were tufts of icing.
Her face seemed to float at the window
wrinkled as the pears drying below her room.

She said she couldn't bear the leaf
patterns stamped in butter and glass.
Afternoons, under the carved ceiling
she would cover her eyes.

Stepping outside, Father
coughed, the trowel falling
from his fingers, blade
against stone. The neighbor's
daughter appeared suddenly
with the last of the winter
plums. She was breathless
and plump in a borrowed cloak.
The blade was still warm, she said.
He had been watching the roses breathe under glass.

II

On Vacation a Woman Mistakes Her Leg

On vacation a woman mistakes her leg
for her husband's leg.

Perhaps the clock has been left behind
and an absence of daylight

inhabits the room like a stray that will not
be wakened. The bats come out, aimless

and maybe crazed with the sounds of air.
She wants her husband to fasten the screen.

He rises, walks awhile under the pines
and the moon, the legendary moon, asking himself

if he is brave. At dawn the invisible lake
glitters again. He guides the boat by the

sun, in circles, while she watches a line of trees
unravel behind his ear. Across the bay

a fisherman thinks they are watching
one another's lips, as he would do

if he were driving a lady in circles.
He thinks they are pink, and damp

with lotion under their flowered shirts.
They do not mention the clouds of shy minnows.

And later they step from bathing suits,
their false bodies on the pine floor.

Their windows pull the lake
right into the room. In their tumblers

the ice can be heard across a mile of water
where a farmer coming home notices the glass

animals his wife has set on the sill.

Ceremony

to Robyn

The colors were green and violet.
She carried them from the lake

into dress after dress and on trains
to the city. All those years

the organist waited, his hands like clouds
above the keys.

Someone presented the veil, the explosion
of flowers, and she watched the last of herself

fade into the gown. The music
began. The histories of those present

rose & disappeared. She
listened, the hair loosening,

the gown flowing perfectly
around her body.

His Early and Late Paintings

His first painting spoke:
the woman had forgotten many lovers

but none of the rooms in which she awoke.
He discarded the armoire and the child's hoop.

He was taken by her hands
and the clay fragments by the bed

and the way the vase left her hands.

His later paintings had no titles:
1. Did his grandchildren tell him what they dreamed?

2. Was there a dispute between peddlers outside his window?
3. Was he thinking of his death?

4. Was the woman later recognized?
At least one observer was startled

to find himself startled.
5. The woman who loved grapes.

6. The woman who spilled wine
abruptly as she left the table.

Rain

The slaves are dragging the last
bundles of figs
to higher ground. These figs
were to sweeten

and be passed among dignitaries.
The king's children
splash at the edge of the new ocean.
A man will walk here again

carrying a map.
He will let out his breath
suddenly. He will wrap
in a piece of soft cloth

a wedge of clay
from which all hair was pressed,
whose figs were eaten and eaten

and whose last
children, standing
on its last visible rise
sat down, tucking their

long shirts beneath them.
Their tutors must already know the story:
why else do they

rush from room to room
in the darkened
palace, not wondering,
talking of lamps, oil, and salt?

Eventually, You

come to a full stop.
This window full of other windows,
this room full of people
who pass daily through the light
and shadows of this view
began as a repetition
of enclosure.

All day the road flowed out of itself,
pulling you past what might have been
good country. The lawns, the curtains,
a family seated in a window
rose and fell back
like rooms remembered by children.
At each stop your legs unbent slowly.

This morning you woke
in the woods where you hid
for years. The nights drew light
from the house you lived in.
You visited each neighbor
once, planning a history
of reunions.

Routes

They left the limbs of the ancestors
tangled in the ground.
Carried their names from low rooms
and from trees that belonged in that
soil, that soft rain.
They rose in mid-sentence
leaving the neighbor's daughters
growing toward their mothers' faces
and the sons listening to old stories.
The names began again
on storefronts, mailboxes
in a country of bare surfaces.
They watched a little money move
easily. Some small trees appeared

and small appliances.
An ocean faded behind the lids
of the oldest men. Strudels
cooled on the eve of each wedding.
Some nights of wind, of leaves
mingling, made the women untie their hair.
And the children rose
from family dinners, speaking the tongue
their fathers learned late,
traveling inland
in cars of the steel that arrived
each year, their names
strange sounds along the highway.

By Surprise

for my grandfather

Chokeberries shrink along the hedge, still
glowing. The slugs that swelled all summer
have curled and dried in their tracks.
There's a nip in the air,
you say, and maybe you mean *the dark house*
pulls us like children, inside at night.

All afternoon you filled your arms
with leaves. Before my time
you set each birch
into the woods, sweating and taking
your time. Your daughters slept, played
and grew lovely, people said,
and sometimes you touched their faces.
This afternoon I watched the paths
keeping their shape beneath you.

The sun this far north, this time of
year, thins early, is little more
than light. We leave our shoes outside.
And because I am here
and the book you lift, from habit, will
wait, you say, *Let's leave off the light.*

Health

His day spreads out like a city.
He spends it opening

doors. Entering a change
of air. Moving in & out

of natural light. Coming
home, he remembers his body

the hour of the evening meal.
His wife is frying chops.

The grey squares of window
repeat the steam. All day

she's moved among this furniture,
a damp Kleenex in her sleeve,

receiving all sounds through the soft
walls of her head.

Night to her is a change of light
in a room. She sneezes

away from his chair. In bed
sleep will come to him suddenly.

Memo

Touch was all.
Many nights of touch
and only yourself to trust.
Your hands led you
through the caverns of other hands.
You brought nothing from the journeys,
lost nothing each time the mind
took back its roots,
learned nothing
when people withdrew with pieces
of what you thought was heart.
The hands set out plates, opened cans.
Your age arrived, one corner
at a time. The familiar hungers turned
their backs. Only the hands
kept up with you,
folding the loose garments,
fingering the sheets
on the thin bed, showing more and more
of their frame, their muscle.

Undressing

First he noticed my
face, he said.

At a distance
the bones surfaced,

they split the light
into pools of no light

and my hair, he said,
so colorless

yet full of breath.
He would walk

into it, he said.
He would disappear.

I undressed for him,
the room so familiar

it contained no odors.
The white walls,

their shadows in place
fell away, and my body

emerged as space
shaped like a body.

Reunions

Someone you haven't seen in years
pulls you inside.

You wonder if you've changed.
You step out of new garments,

a premonition of loss. He snuffs the candle
he will take with him, and you slip into something

safe: a dream of antelope or horses
pressing against each other.

Later it's your husband
who removes your coat. You know this room

and the names no one has spoken.
A woman is pregnant, waving her cigarette

like a summons.

Integumentary

I

Keep a hand on your manners
and the shape of each day that approaches.
If you cannot cover a question with words
you let it ask you too much.
Avoid dealing in distance: you've gone too far
if you can't find your way back on the sound
of your voice. Other points:
release expression evenly
among your features, and gather no more
of an object that has never been yours
than you can carry in one hand.

II

The notion of stopping
drains from your mind.
You may be someone you met somewhere,
you can no longer tell.
Each palm accepts outlines of pebbles,
your skin divides into delicate bruises.
You no longer know a difference
between question and travel;
you could weave yourself into any location
if you stayed long enough.
You court everything.
You pull out words
where you can. Wherever you reach
you touch a cheek, a chin, a wild eye
you've known well.

Money

Now you appear,
oddly wrapped in air
and glass. The walls smell

of lemon, or marble, of plants
that live for weeks without water.
The absent woman's breath

silvers the ear. Elsewhere
she unhooks an earring, not
thinking of money, the stillness

of these rooms, or the child
who isn't here.
You barely hear

your bus in the distance purring,
its cargo of fretful babies.
You open another magazine

in which another house is lovely
and silent as it seems.
The occupant is resting in her

other home. You are running
your hand again
across the highly polished lawn.

Waiting

I come home with a huge picture of
myself which I hang in the kitchen.

I listen to myself. My words have become
music. I promise myself everything.

And if the decision goes against me
will I hear them let out their breath?

Will I know the exact moment
before their eyes my image disappears?

Will their chairs squeak?
Are these my hands dangling like fruit?

2

I only dream of myself angry enough.
In the next room someone howls and breaks

glass. I stick to Victorian novels: Step-
ping from the carriage, a young squire

articulates his confusion; his dilemma
suspends itself in the leaves overhead.

I look up from my book and there's snow.
I look up from my book and a celebration

has begun in a lamplit corner of this
room. Where would I find a plumed pen?

L'Étreinte

How large he is.

So much flesh and sparse
hair. I press him here

and here, until I learn
the shape of him well

enough to carry into the street
and back. The walls behind him

are endless as night through a train
window, and I am the child pressed

at the glass, pressed into miles
of land. I want to be my mother

who had herself for shelter.
Later I'll say his name

the way I used to gather
stones and broken glass

and forget them
and let them grow warm in my hands.

Shade

You never saw your mother's
body, only a face
which fades now without
disappearing, like the saints'
faces in silver. And the nuns,
the sisters you might have
kept—they knelt and rose
as though made of air. Where
did their legs begin?
They gathered their skirts
like girls. And you took no food
without their blessing.
Now you must think before rising:
I went to him without
thinking. I touched him everywhere.
Within the folds of their skirts
the nuns rose as though wearing nothing.
They rose as though leaving their bodies.
Already the sun grows
and you rise, porous
with sleep, and sweating.
He makes room as you pass.
You remember how the leaves in midsummer
clouded the stained glass,
and the litanies—
the murmuring of their voices
like insects moving into the shade.

Dancing

At dawn, I begin
at the window, unable to begin

in the flesh-colored light.
At night I am singular

and white in my multiple names;

I can turn each of my bones
to air.

I can take the trembling,
when it begins, deep inside

like a gypsy swallowing flame.

I've heard that men
are frightened of my body,

that they conjure it in the dark
over women they've made into wives.

My last lover never closed his eyes.

Magnificent, he said carefully
as though I were water

and he a swan poised
over a swan's image.

Lately, now, the bed tilts

while I sleep. By morning
I'm stiff, endangered

like some parchments.
The child I may never have

rises, plump with sleep;

my thoughts lurch
backward, straining

for purchase,
resume their necessary flow.